DUB WISE

ALSO BY GEOFFREY PHILP

Poetry
Exodus
Florida Bound
Hurricane Center
Xango Music
Twelve Poems and a Story for Christmas

Fiction
Uncle Obadiah and the Alien
Benjamin, My Son
Who's Your Daddy & Other Stories

Children's writing
Grandpa Sydney's Anancy Stories

Give thanks to the following publications in which some of these poems have been published: *MiPoesias, Concelebratory Shoehorn Review, Picolata Review, The Caribbean Writer, Asili, Dance the Guns to Silence, Ann Arbor Review, Canopic Jar, Julie Mango: Online Journal of Creative Expressions, Peony Moon, Ocho, St. Somewhere, tongues of the ocean* and *So Much Things To Say.*

Give thanks also to Kamau Brathwaite, Olive Senior, Mervyn Morris, Lorna Goodison, Emma Trelles, Opal Palmer Adisa, and Pam Mordecai for their help and guidance with the editing of these poems. Your suggestions have helped to make *Dub Wise* a better book.

GEOFFREY PHILP

DUB WISE

P E E P A L   T R E E

First published in Great Britain in 2010
Peepal Tree Press Ltd
17 King's Avenue
Leeds LS6 1QS
UK

ISBN 13: 9781845231712

Supported by
**ARTS COUNCIL
ENGLAND**

CONTENTS

For Nadia
Anna, Christina and Andrew

POEMS FOR THE INNOCENT

FATHER POEM

Tonight when the moon forgives darkness,
and peers through a curtain of leaves,

she will skitter to the end of the block,
her laughter kissing the tops of blossoms

dozing on folded petals of bougainvilleas
whose thorns surrender to night,

preferring to accept dew on their tips
and muse at the transparent world

in the breath of my children against the pane,
waiting for the familiar grunt of my engine

turning up our driveway from the sodium dervish
of the highway and into bliss of their outstretched arms.

TALLAHASSEE 2005

On those cold mornings when my daughter
shuttled between work and classes, she'd bury
her face in her sweater as her bus heaved a steady

sigh around the circle named for Chief Osceola,
who spent his final hours in a dry cell, dreaming
of the day when his people would remember

old stories that reminded them who they were
before the advent of musket and small pox,
before they learned words like "cannon"

and forgot their own names;
before he was betrayed by his own nobility,
for believing the war could ever end –

seeing friends when he should have counted enemies;
captured under a white flag,
whipped by the wind, like the scarves

of those old black men she saw along side
roads of Tallahassee, bent by work and promises,
like angels in the mist, stumbling home before first light.

SUMMER STORM

After thunderstorms have cleared the city,
after the homeless have abandoned their cardboard palaces,

fog older than Tequesta circles, Seminole arrowheads
and Spanish jars, dulls the sawgrass's razor,

turns away from charted rivers,
slithers over the boulevard I could not cross

when the names Lozano and McDuffie rhymed
with necklaces of burning tires, and away

from churches with broken steeples that grow
more vacant each Sunday because their faithful

folded their arms while *balseros* floundered, *boriquas*
drowned, and *neg* joined their sisters and brothers

on the ocean bed. Yet something like music
rises from the sound of gull's wings beating a path

over Calle Ocho, Little Haiti, *La Sawacera*, like bells
that echo over the Freedom Tower, bright as the final

burst of the sunset against billboards, gilding the sea
grapes' leaves washed clean by evening rain.

BODHISATTVAS

(In memory of the New York firefighters)
For Lisa Berman-Shaw

Wherever there are sentient
beings in need of compassion,
sick in need of comfort,
hungry in need of food, they arise,
summoned by cries of innocents
to awaken the bounty of our sleeping
lives, and they cannot rest
until stones find solace.

So when we were strapped securely
in our SUVs in Key West, Van Buren, Providence,
Nome, chugging money like Saudi oil,
thinking we were safe in our towers
of steel and glass, cages of mortality
that turned to smoke, ash, soot —
they did what they have always
done through time and space,
dropped their lives and snatched us
from the midst of the fire.

DANCING WITH KATRINA

(*For Kalamu ya Salaam*)

Paddling through New Orleans,
past a shotgun house up to its threshold
in brine, a dog, paws folded, waits
on the roof of his owner's drowned
home, stares across the river
at splintered houses in the shade
of pines, swaying in the wind
that keeled those sailboats
in the bay, leaning on each other
like partygoers after Mardi Gras.

The laughter of that Creole
lady bright as Louis Armstrong's
horn, that gave birth to this city,
rises above the stench of mildew
and rot, as she puts on her torn
stockings, so that when the waters go,
as they will, she will be ready to work
as she has always worked – with style,
she will be ready to live as she has always
lived – with love, and she'll be ready
to dance with her stilettos in the mud.

September 10, 2005

ESTIMATED PROPHET: VERSION

*"The second angel poured out his bowl into the sea, and it became blood
like that of a dead man; and every living thing in the sea died."*
                                    Revelation 16:3, King James Version.

Our prophets have abandoned us to our lies.
They've packed spare clothes, retreated to the Mojave
where they can still bless wild, untamed spaces,
praise the elation of kestrels, their aerial dance
away from smoke that poisons the brave,
threads a man's lungs and veins with fine lace,
sweetens a mother's milk that darkens her firstborn's eyes;
rattlers coiled under a Joshua tree have a better chance.
And it's no use begging like televangelists for them to come back;
who'd want to listen to them on the "burning shore" anyway?
Everyone knows true holy lands are way across the sea
and you can't Twitter prophecy any more than you can save
pelicans from the spray of dispersants or mangroves from an oil slick.
No, better to mortgage our dreams. At least, that's what the voices say.

ERZULIE'S DAUGHTER

It began with the usual insults
about her nose and hips,
and the belief that her true-true mother
lived on a coral island protected
by sunken galleys and man-o-wars.

These fantasies,
her therapists said, were drawing her
toward a different future
than her parents had wished for
when they punished her
for not reading the books they'd studied,
and sent her away on Easter egg hunts
dressed in starched, pink dresses, white bonnets,
and blue bows in each braid of her stubborn hair.

And when she began cutting her wrists,
arms, legs, and belly, her parents
agreed with the psychiatrists
to the prescriptions of pills, potions,
and poisons to keep her grounded in this life.

But then, the scabs became scars became scales,
her hair grew wild and untamed,
and a garden of yellows, blues, and reds sprouted
on her arms, legs, and back –
her ears and lips studded with gold –
and almost overnight she changed into something
she had always resembled in her own dreams,
in the mirror of her mother –
something beautiful and fearsome.

MARASSA JUMEAUX

Already offerings of candy and toys
have been spread at our feet to appease,
but we had no part in this. So many souls

did not have to join our ancestors.
Bondye has given you the power to save
yourselves, but like those priests who pretend

they don't know we are older than their god;
presidents who sold blood for pearls as smooth
as skulls that hang around Michelle's neck;

poets who would not speak in their mother's
tongue, but remained mute as mulattos
who banned the name Papa Dessalines;

nèg refuse to see the fault that runs
deep through the chains of these islands,
betrayals that not even Maman *Défilé*

could heal. So bury us soon, for although
the earth is young, this island has been shaking
since the saints awakened at *Bois Caiman.*

Put our tiny bones in the caves of Jacmel,
under the waterfalls of Cormier Plage,
erect headstones from crushed cement

and twisted rebar to rebuild the dream,
for there is one who has always stood between us
in whose presence we tremble.

LIMBO: VERSION

(For Kamau Brathwaite)

Spirit flashes down the spine of twin
crosses that hold my body, yet free
my arms to undulate through time

until I am as small as a spider;
drums pull me under the tide
that has borne so many back to Guinee,

and I bend my legs on the sand
of this new world baptized by blood,
inch toward space crowned

by torch light and hushed voices
on the other side of the auction block
welcoming with uncertain music

of kete and fife, alive and chained
with the promise to my brother, my father:
Atibon Legba, ouvrir barriere pour nous . . .

GATHERING OF THE GODS: MIAMI 2010

The six o'clock train, emissary of Ogun

whistles through West Dixie, the meandering

line that divides Miami, while my daughter

cruises through amber haze and I lisp

my entreaty to the orishas to keep her safe

from flying metal: SUVs that do not heed

Xango's wrath nor Erzulie's love, but hurl

through Eleggua's X, ignorant of his plea

not for blood, but for the respect as the first

to speak in front of the infinite silence

of Olódùmarè who lives in the space

between box cars and kyries of eagles.

A KIND OF SURRENDER
(*For H.*)

Like some Greek heroine –
she would accept the dare
born from the fissure
between those whom she had loved –
the fault lines that unearthed fists
of pine that ringed wetlands, forests
of hardwood hammocks, and sinkholes
further north – and she would swallow
those hard white tablets, one
by one – while the pouis blared
their yellow trumpets against the Lenten
sky patched by a pale promise –
Azrael's hands spread between his luminous
wings, as he gently squeezed her heart –
a bitter pill for every year

(ii)

There are evenings like this
when I understand why she slipped
from this life, desiring neither hell
nor heaven, no longer wanting to carry
the burden of becoming someone else's lover,
wife, mistress, to just fall asleep
and let dreams analyse
her choices: the bad ones
that in time would look like wisdom;
the good ones that led to the bedroom
pillow, the stifled screams.

Yet downstairs, I hear the gurgle
of my neighbour's newborn, the thump
of my son playing basketball with some kid
from down the street, my daughter dancing
to "*Habibi, habibi*", and I turn away
from the bathroom cabinet, chalk
pills and tumbler of water, the tap left running,
and welcome back my loves
to whom I had become a stranger, arguing
in the hallway, murmuring
in the living room, asleep on the verandah.

ALL SUICIDES

are cowards, little sister, for they've lost faith
in this rhythm that sustains through drought
and storm – in the surety of the sun trailing
off sofas, prickling hairs of Spanish
needles clinging to bark of the umbrella tree,
over knives of the bromeliad cutting back night –
that remind us, this earth, in time, will right herself.

Pull back, little sister, leave the image
of the girl in the shattered mirror, and follow
the woman by the door beckoning you to go deeper
into the wilderness where you are,
and where we are made whole again.

Pull back, little sister, call my name
through the darkness – say, "I am",
for you have suffered too long and alone;
walk through these doors,
touch my forehead; I will awaken
before the light leaves your face.

A POEM FOR THE INNOCENTS

A killing moon peeks through leaves
of trumpet trees in full bloom
for Lent, their barks crisscrossed
by wild strokes of a machete
when my son tried to help me weed
our garden, overrun with dandelions,
branches, leaves, a bounty of seed
and thorns, side by side, under clusters
of suns bursting through the branches.

Shadows flicker across the wall upstairs,
over Buzz Lightyear's grin, Mr. Potato
Head's sigh, and under a map
dotted with cities that fill his dreams.

What promises will I make
when I climb the stairs
before he falls asleep to the noise
of the television with cluster
bombs blooming in the sky
over Baghdad? What comfort
can I give him as I draw the sheets
over his shoulders, kiss his forehead,
when he worries that if he closes his eyes,
his Aunt Batsheva, half a world away,
will not rise from her bed in Gan Yavne,
thirty-seven miles west of Ramah
where Rachel wept for her children
and refused to be comforted.

The map over his bed now frightens
him, and I cannot convince him,
despite the miles and miles of oceans
and deserts, that the machete

under his bed will not make him safer,
any more than the sacrifice of innocents
will save us, for he knows,
he knows, somewhere
between the Tigris and Euphrates,
a wave of steel races toward Babylon.

March 22, 2003

IBISES

This evening I am greeted by a swarm
of police cars among bleached notes
of foreclosure on my neighbour's lawn.

Red and blue lights almost blind me
to yellow tape and lifting wings of ibises
digging for rumour and insects in wet grass

blackened by grunts of SUVs
lumbering towards traffic
flowing under a sickle moon

that binds this earth with one promise
as she catches the tails of overhead
cargo planes – raw music of the city

muting my prayer as I drag my shadow
up the driveway, open my door to the usual
talk of mortgage and money:

"Let there be peace in this house.
Lord, let there be peace in this house."

CREATION

"In my beginning is my end."
"East Coker" by T.S. Eliot

Sunday before first light, I am hurtling down US1, not wanting to return to that place of so many defeats.

I am sleeping in a bed beside my lover, listening to her breathe; her arms caress the pillow and her legs wrap the sheets. I come back between cramped lanes that arrow toward white space like the voices that bleed from the nib of my pen – how to say this or that – how to make sense of the darkness on either side of my bed: the words that have no name – fatherless as I once was – fathered and a father as I am now.

Then, the turning and tearing, the refusal to say this or that – the rage at the dark blot of lies in every spot on the pad – like a man who has betrayed his lover and searches the alleys of his neighbourhood – why this happened or that – to find why she said this or he did that. He awakens in the middle of a dream, smelling of rum and cigarettes, not sure of where he was, who he was with, or where he is going. And out of habit, he turns the key and the engine, which thankfully, answers, and the sodium lights allow him to see, just barely, what he knows lies beyond the hood of his car.

I roll down the windows, listen to the slap of the tires against the asphalt – the ones I should have replaced months ago, but I'm still too broke to fix – turn on the AM radio hoping to find an old song that will make me cry like I used to, and watch, with fear on my breath, gulls descend on a parking lot beside the beach.

DUB WISE

DUB WISE

Between the sizzle of the high hat,
thump of backbeat, this insistence
that curls tendrils of wild yam
and opens dry flowers of sarcoma –
inhuman beauty from which I can neither
turn away, nor praise – like that moment
on my grandfather's farm when I knew
a terrible joy – spaces larger than a lifetime
of worry would ever understand,
choices made for love
neither asked nor offered,
forgiveness sure as the river's trail
in my hands – fluid as the sap of poinsettias
that bled all winter – when I entered the stream
that held me close as I went deeper,

deeper.

¿COMO SE DICE ESO?
(For Nadia)

¿Como se dice eso? How do I
say this? The hollow feel of pillows
against the headboard familiar as the green
of St. Ann, *el calor del mar de Progreso*, the cold
pews of Sacre Coeur, lost as the light
in these photographs, like the taste
of the small hairs under your navel?

¿Como se dice eso? How do I say
this? That I will never go back
to those cane fields that share
the mockingbird's trill with my grandfather's
voice that has become one with the fog
rising over fishing boats before the moon
covers herself behind mountains
– far away as your body is from mine.

¿Como se dice eso? How do I say this?
That I have lied to you, lied to myself,
and I've learned this awful truth –
that heaven is everywhere.
For I have known these places:
the way light gilds the altar of Sacre
Coeur; the way guava trees in St Ann hold
morning dew on the backs of their leaves;
the way dolphins at Progreso swam with us
into the ocean; the way I have loved your body.

SUMMER LOVE
(*For Nadia*)

"And summer's lease hath all too short a date."
— Sonnet XVIII — William Shakespeare

When evening ambles down Flagler
to the tumble of closing cash registers,
mould of faded bills in the back
pocket of his blue, pin-striped suit,
she will go with him only as far
as the river to watch fishing
boats with their tail of terns and pelicans
flashing wings, like silver,
against glass vaults of Brickell.

But when night struts along Biscayne
with the rumble of reggae in his stride,
tabaco and *mojitos* on his breath,
desire tight around his waist,
she will lead him down the causeway
into cooling waters of the bay,
daily cares sliding off their flesh,
and her dark laughter, like waves,
lapping the sides of the Rickenbacker.

PRELUDE

Watching these pelicans
in a moment change from their aerial
grace into killers – chopping
fish that dart in and out of coral
ships inert on the ocean bed –
recovering from the night's hangover
when fog drifted above the sea's slate
writing her name over and over
like a teenage girl's first love –
the way we write our life
into the lives of those whom we've loved –
lapping and overlapping like a net
of dreams, or the way our bodies hold
themselves, pressing each moment
until space collapses into a pinpoint
of light, from which we emerge,

                              untouched.

REST POEM

My sister drags her shadow across
the back of Miami Avenue, her head
brewed in wood smoke, fingers
knotted around the smell of money.

Rest, little sister.

Leave the money in the till, uncounted,
rumpled beds, unmade,
dust in the corners, unswept

Rest, little sister.

Rest, your head on the cushion of my shoulder,
your arms on the pillow of my chest,
your feet in the cradle of my lap.

Rest, little sister, rest.

BACHATA

(For Nadia)

After every party in our house
when reggae, reggaeton, R&B
have exhausted younger couples,
and they sit separately to cool down,
I want to dance with you,
the way our friends, Miguel and Ramona,
who have made a promise,
that despite their struggle
with lawyers, bill collectors, and cancer,
they will never leave each other.
And whenever the bachata begins –
we stop to watch how
he will catch her –
she spins out of his arm's reach,
they pass like strangers,
but then his hand
finds the small of her back,
her legs quiver to the old music,
and they are partners in time
with the rhythm, once more.

POETRY WOMAN

From the back of her throat to the perfect O
of her mouth, she traces a lineage
to the first cry in the hold

when the women who carried the seed of the Akan
across an ocean that changed their names
from a welcome sound christened by drums

to a grunt at the foot of a sugar mill;
then, a low moan as if the scream
cannot escape the prison of her breath,

between her teeth and pink tongue,
to become itself, and not something of air
and darkness, as light wraps

around her waist the way her voice holds
ancient secrets to baptize the word
like a mother's caress of her firstborn's

face, adoring each gurgle
fresh from the lips of God, like chants
of those sisters cascading from the rafters

on Sundays, to their moans on the dancehall
floor on Saturdays – and can still laugh
from the sweetness, the sweetness of it all.

BEYOND MOUNTAIN VIEW

ODE TO BROTHER JOE: VERSION

(For Tony McNeill)

Brother Joe get arrested
for crack this time and the police
nah jester. Them say it a go on
too long. Brother Joe a bruk
the law like him is Marcus Garvey,
so them haul him off to the lockup.

Brother Joe get salt, for neither him don
nor him senator going save him, so it lef
as usual to him woman
to find the bail money before the police
beat Brother Joe inna the ground,
or till they say Brother Joe get crass,
attack the sergeant with a sharp straw,
and them haffi shat him.

And the brethren still burning
the weed and beating the drums,
reading and chanting from Isaiah,
searching for a sign of the new messiah
to rescue Brother Joe, the island, the whole
race, while Brother Joe holding on,
bleeding in him cell, still believing
that him life is fulfillmant of the book,
and we and him watching and waiting
for the door to open — still catching hell.

FOR BROTHER BOB

Again and again, I heard your voice,
whispering through the noise, "Don't cry. Just sing."
In dregs of a bottle thinking I didn't have a choice,
again and again, I heard your voice.

When I felt even my bones were cursed,
and my body trembled from the troubles Babylon can bring,
again and again, I heard your voice,
whispering through the noise, "Don't cry. Just sing."

MULE TRAIN: VERSION

Lawd, me know it wrong,
but, do, doan mek de boots
buss, fa me an de pickney
cyaan tek no more. Fa yu know
de reason I mek de deal
fe carry dis poison
inna me belly an heart.

Ev'ry mornin' me an de pickney
wake up from sleeping pon de col'
floor, an me haffi clean dem eye,
wipe way de matta, send dem
go school with jus a prayer
inna me heart
that so fassy-fassy now
is like smady close de door
inna me ches', an lef me one
fe walla naked in de dus'.

Lawd, do, I know I shud trus'
only you, but dis plastic
is de one t'ing dat stan'
between me and certain deat'
an t'ings not looking
so good wid de acid bubblin'
up me throat an unda me tongue
an I wonderin' even if I mek it,
how I gwine live?

CONFESSION

The old man came into my grandfather's
shop and I ignored him when he sat on the barrels
of mackerel, the air heavy with cheese and salt.
"You're too young to remember, but I going tell
about a Jamaica that never existed,
yet I was there: a place where man and man
lived side by side, yet hated each other;
where you could poke seeds in the ground
and in two-twos there would be trees
with the sweetest fruit, yet people were hungry;
a place of fresh water springs bubbling
out of the ever-giving earth, yet people were thirsty;
a time and a place of pastries and puddings
and every earthly delight, yet people
had no joy." That's when I told him to stop,
but he wouldn't. "All who can't hear must feel,"
is what my father always said.
"Why you torturing me with these fantasies?"
"Because you must know."
That's when I hit the bugger. I beat him.
I beat him and I beat him until he was cold,
so he wouldn't tell any more lies. And on my life,
Officer, every word I tell you is true.

WARNER WOMAN: VERSION

(For Edward Baugh)

She came, they say, wearing a dress as red
as the dirt of the countryside, and stood
at the crossroads of Matilda's Corner
shaking her fists at mansions
on the hills: "The Spirit descended on me
to speak these words to the nation,
for they have wandered in paths
that I have not taught them.
And I have heard cries of widows
and orphans in the streets, but the wicked
who fear neither flood nor famine,
and have built their fortresses, their walled
communities and garrisons, have said,
'Who is there like us to judge us?'
But thus sayeth the Lord of Hosts,
'Kingston, O Kingston, how I would have loved
to have gathered you to my bosom
the way the sea caresses the shore.
But you have preferred storm and hurricane.
So, I say, woe to you for you have slaughtered
my children, the old, and the crippled.
Woe to you, for you have stoned and exiled
my prophets. Woe to you, for you have defrauded
the homeless and the poor." Then she ripped
her dress in two, spat on the asphalt three times,
and ran like a horse without its rider,
back up to Long Mountain, up into the darkness
gathering around the tops of trees
with the smell of rain around their roots.

DIARY OF A MAD EVANGELIST

Even that man who lives on a far hill,
whose wife, a Delilah, paints her face,

tempts all the boys at the grocery store
until they have had their fill with her body

that reeks from oils and perfumes –
sin that has risen like smoke from scorched

bones to clot the nostrils of God –
their fornications and adulteries have not

gone unnoticed. Not one
will be spared, not even the whimpering

dog that sits by the window, gazing out
into the yard. For haven't we suffered enough

for a remnant who've always disobeyed
the law – when only the whip could teach

us the Word? Like Samson, I will wipe out
iniquity, decorate the trees with their bodies

to forestall the greater wrath that will catch –
like those slave ships – those who have fallen

asleep on their watch at the hour of the Lord
of Hosts, coming like a thief in the night.

LETTER FROM MARCUS GARVEY
London, 9 June 1940

When I was in the Atlanta Federal Prison
I chanted through the silence, "Keep cool,
keep cool," for I didn't want to see twisted
bodies ripening on the flowering dogwood.

Or when I emerged from the caverns
of the Spanish Town District Prison,
the children hurled stones at my head,
like I was some lame poet,
and even after my first betrayal
when Amy brawled with a Judas,
you ignored me, and said I made us
"a laughingstock to the world."

I took it, because I knew you were blind
to your own beauty, that you could be seduced
by weak-kneed hypocrites who would call me
"a half-wit, low-grade moron." I took it all.
But what has me choking on my words,
is not the asthma, the shortness of breath
that has slowed my heart, my body
that will be taken away soon-soon
by the whirlwind – what's left me mute
is the broken faith of my brothers
and sisters, scattered like goats
on a far hillside where my father lies
buried under the broad leaves of the breadfruit:
his bones warmer than these cold
white pages swirling in my doorway.

BEYOND MOUNTAIN VIEW

As we descend Mountain View Avenue,
past houses that lie prone
beneath Wareika, scarred by hurricanes
and bulldozers, past walls
smeared with graffiti that still divide the city,
I roll up my window from the stench
of the sea at low tide that creeps
into storefronts and rum bars,
into the hair of sisters in floral
prints, shirts of brothers
with spliffs tucked behind their ears,
up the legs of children rolling
spokeless bicycle rims down a lane
still unchanged by my love,
and ready myself for the blinding blue
of the Caribbean Sea that shapes
the palisades of Kingston, shrubbed
by mangroves and sea grapes, round
the bend that in my childhood led
to Harbour View, away from my father's
anger, as light flashes outside
my window, across my driver's face,
making even the bush beautiful.

Near the roundabout, our car joins
a line of holiday traffic heading
toward the airport, smell of the dead
harbour clinging to my body,
and a man, armed with a rake and machete,
clears debris from the embankments,
branches that block signs for travellers like me
who have forgotten which side of the road leads home.

RED

It burst from those lips that I'd loved, "You're just too red!"
The curse of being apart, neither black nor white, but red

followed me through streets, staining the shadow
of those fires that flared behind my mother's garden – red

ginger towering over anthuriums with their bruised phalloi
straining against the bark of the live oak, stunned red

petals bending in sunlight to the weight of shame,
their pliant skin absorbing yellow and blue to become red,

like the way by resisting we become the thing we fear most –
as I now accept this blessing freed from race. Call me Red.

WRITING LIFE SESTINA

When rejections pile up, and I begin to hate my writing,
sometimes I think I'd be better off selling weed.
With my colour and accent, I'm a natural.
I've already got a corner on the market.
All I'd have to do is screw up my face, grow dreads,
and buy a gun, so I'd look like a "real Jamaican".

But what does it mean to be a real Jamaican?
I know for sure it doesn't involve writing.
I'd make more money as a Rastitute or rent-a dread,
selling my body to tourists and smoking weed.
It would be a much better way to get on TV or market
myself. I'd get up every morning singing, "There's a natural

mystic blowin' through the air… such a natural
mystic." I'd become a famous reggae star with a huge Jamaican
fan club. I could even sing, "Carry me ganja go a Linstead Market."
My audience would love it! Then, I could go back to writing
every day and use my advance to buy some good weed,
and take a picture for the back cover of the book with dreads

(or fake ones) covering my face with my all dread
football team: "Rasta All Stars". And we'd eat only natural
foods, and when we'd get hungry, smoke like a ton of weed.
We'd make red, green, and gold t-shirts – the real Jamaican
colours. I could make more money selling t-shirts than writing,
and wasting my money every year on *Poet's Market*.

Who am I kidding trying to sell this stuff? The only way to market
Caribbean poetry is to write about how the times are dread,
and how the white man makes life hard. Nobody publishes writing
that sounds like Walcott, except if it's really Walcott, who's a natural
poet, but he's from St. Lucia – though he's been labelled a Jamaican
because he's a known ladies' man, but he's never smoked weed.

Or has he? How could he have written *Omeros* without smoking weed?
Walcott could do commercials for ganja – a whole new way to market
sensi as a cure for writer's block: picture yourself on a Jamaican
beach with a big spliff in your mouth, girls stroking your dreads
and all the while you are rocking in a hammock to the natural
"Sounds from the Island" – the formula to improve anyone's writing!

But it won't work. It's easier to grow dreads and look natural,
than trying to market poetry by a Jamaican baldhead.
But just to hedge my bets, I'm sticking to writing (and smoking weed.)

CALABASH POEM

It began innocently when Kwame, Colin and me was to read;
smady shout out, "Oonu cyaan write! Oonu mus a smoke weed!"
Then, a next one, "Do you know Latin or Greek? I doubt if you can even spell."
We was on JBC-TV, so we couldn't say, "Man, fuck off. Go to hell!"
Still, we couldn't take it like that; we had honour, we had to save face.
I said, "We know we're the best! Meet us on the field, any time, any place!
A week from now, a duel of scrimmage, three man to a side,
to prove the best writers in JA, or make it better, world wide!"
For nowadays you can't judge a writer's worth just by the size
of royalties, NEA fellowships or even the Pulitzer prize.
Nobody reads any more, and everything depends
on your agent or if you're sleeping with your editor's best friend.

Still, not a soul answer the challenge, not one take the bet,
even when we send it far and wide, all over the Internet.
Ondaatje, Rushdie, and Coetzee say they didn't have the time,
we said, "Make way, boys. You're history and way past your prime."
Then Caryl Phillips, David Dabydeen and Austin Clarke came in pads,
dressed to play cricket, and they really looked sad
when we said we'd never play that game again, those days were done,
Babylon had fallen with the empire's setting sun.
It was good we never played them; they'd have beat us for sure,
but all's fair in writing, in love, and in war.
But when people test you, and draw a line in the sand,
you have to tip the scales and play your best hand.
America teach us that – don't hang on to the past.
Fairness doesn't count. Nice guys finish last!
The deadline came, we'd won our own cup.
We'd won by default, for not a single writer or critic showed up.
We were the best in the world; we was rolling in the grass,
but then we looked up: it was Naipaul, Brathwaite, and Walcott to raas.

We started to worry, we started to fret, but Kwame said we couldn't lose,
"I'm also a critic, even if they win, we'll have better reviews!"

Kwame told them, "We respect you, but now you're too old to fight
and it really wouldn't be fair, you three elders taught us how to write!"
Brathwaite and Naipaul agreed, they didn't want to do anything rash,
but Walcott wouldn't let it go – you'd think we were playing for cash!

We changed into jerseys that Colin supplied us for free,
Random House was sponsoring us from *Waiting in Vain's* royalties.
We wondered who'd sponsor these codgers who were now old and grey,
for we don't' support our writers – and forget it if you're gay!
But these stalwarts were shrewd and still showed their wort',
ads for Viagra and Prozac were plastered all over their shirts.

Lawd, God, people don't get mad, is only a joke.
Sit down and relax, light a spliff, take a little smoke.
We couldn't have a book or be here today –
these men are our heroes despite what Naipaul has to say.
But we had to fight to prove that we, too, were men,
and we was going to see which was mightier, the ball or the pen?

The game start with Colin marking Naipaul on the right,
Kwame with Brathwaite, and me with Walcott in me sight.
The game dragged on for six hours on the beach; it was a battle of wills,
We played long into the night, but the score was nil-nil.

We outplayed them, but as God is my witness, every time we get a chance,
they would make some little comment and throw we off balance.
Colin get an open goal, but Naipaul say, "You think you're a warrior?
All your book is shit. Read bout true man in *The Suffrage of Elvira*!"
Kwame get the ball, but Brathwaite whisper in him ear,
"*Arrivants* is the standard. I never did like your *Progeny of Air*!"
And as him turn to answer that mawga *griot,*
Brathwaite thief way the ball. Them was playing we real low.
As for me, me never say nothing, for me can't even pay my rent,
so how me going match up to *Omeros* or *The Arkansas Testament*?

The game dragged on and we was getting tired,
but with Prozac and Viagra these old boys were totally wired.
Then Walcott get a look in him green eye when the Viagra kick in,
him look like the boy from *Star Apple Kingdom*, the mulatto Shabine.
Walcott rise up like a young stallion, fetlocks pawing the ground –
look like him was going write another *Midsummer* or *Tiepolo's Hound*.
The old men was tiring us out, that was their plan;
we were playing their game, marking them man for man.

A crowd gather and is like we was going faint, but an old dread
bawl out, "Don't falter now, my yout, play hard or dead!"
That's when we perk up; I block Walcott, pass Kwame the ball,
him salad Brathwaite and Colin stand up to Naipaul.
Him shake off the old Indo-Aryan, and left him a rage:
"That's for *A Bend in the River* and *The Middle Passage*!"

Colin scored the goal, and up and down the sideline
girls started to jump and shake they body line.
"We win, we win," we shouted under the lights –
and the three old men trudge proudly into the night.

Still, we felt bad and although we did win,
it was like killing our fathers – it felt like a sin.
But Freud and Bloom say that's how it's always been,
by murdering your father, that's how history begin.

MYSTERIES

MYSTERIES

(For Pam Mordecai)

I still don't know how you surprised
him, and I'm still waiting for an answer
for why you did it – like you
must have been hungry or needed
drugs to feed that other hunger
that vanishes in a cloud of smoke?
But mysteries, like the presence
of the soul, questions about angels,
remain – why did you kill my brother?

Why did mash up his pretty smile,
spill his brains over the back seat
with your gun and bullets,
so I find him with blood over his chest
and arms down to his legs
that used to scamper
down the lane with one tire
and one piece of stick with me
trailing behind him, and we would
pretend that he was the Governor General
and I was the Queen of England,
riding in a limousine to King's House?

And how I wish to God
it could have been like when we played
dandy shandy, and I would throw the ball
so hard, and he would slide away
from the danger like magic,
laughing, "Slip, you fool"
so that when you think you had cornered
him in his car, all you would have heard
was, "Not there. Not there!"

ISAAC'S SACRIFICE

I wonder if he ever spoke to his father
again? I mean, there he was playing
marbles in the dirt with his friends,
or out in the fields flying a kite
while John Crows circled over the tamarinds,
and then his father's familiar bellow,
"Isaac, get the donkey, and stop
with those fool-fool games!
And what have I told you
about playing with those little hooligans
who don't wear any sandals?" But this time
it was different. This time his father was as cross
as a jackass with a burr on its tail.

They climbed the hill without a word
between them, and Isaac gathered the sticks
and bramble, washed himself clean in the cool
springs the way his father had ordered him,
before he left to gather stones...

And when they were both finished,
Abraham, tears in his eyes, asked Isaac
to lie down on a makeshift altar
and being a good son, Isaac obeyed,
even when he saw the long knife
hovering over his chest, and didn't blink,
even as Abraham said, "This is not about God;
it is to teach us who we are."
Then turned, as if he had heard
another voice and found a new sacrifice.

As they descended the hill,
and Isaac was kicking stones
out of the path without Abraham

complaining about ruining his new sandals,
and patting him on the head, saying,
"My boy, my only begotten son,"
trying to be his friend, again,
Isaac probably held Abraham's trembling
hand against his cheek, and forgave him,
yet he couldn't help but think,
"What would have happened
 if the old goat hadn't been so lost?"

JOSEPH AND HIS BROTHERS

(i)

His story began with a lie
when his brothers pushed him
into a pit where he wrestled
with the bones of jackals.
Stripped of the name
he hated, he found himself
interpreting the dreams of a fat man
in a barren land, accused
of a crime that he had desired.

But in her room, Joseph had a vision
of those who'd gone before him –
scorpions and bed bugs writhing
between her sheets – and he bolted,
yet left enough evidence
to encourage *su-su* and Potiphar's
hatred: Joseph had seen his nakedness
and fled his wife's clammy cage,
so Potiphar rewarded him
with a mustier cell among thieves and liars.

Yet Joseph wished himself away
to the palace to decipher shadows
that disturbed the king's evening nap
when the drowsing sun gave colour
to purple grapes in his vineyard,
drowned in the muddy river.

And after so many years in the dark,
Joseph saw the promise of famine
in the king's cheeks, the bounty
between his palms, and dreamt
himself Lord of the Nile.

(ii)

Mumbling threats into their beards,
the murderers said the old man
was barely alive after they took
Benjamin, his youngest, born
from his beloved's final breath
before she passed into the stillness
that Joseph imagined, as his father
raised his blind eyes to the red sun
rising over khaki dunes, and with dust
on his lips, yearned for that silence,
but not willing to go, not yet.

For something in his bones kept telling him
the story of the tribe was not over,
that someone would come and figure out,
the meaning of this scattering to the wind,
make sense of the missing parts of the tale –
why this happened or why she had to die
so young and leave him for so long,
for someone to whisper her name
that echoed in the shell of his ear.

(iii)

Joseph steadied himself in the antechamber.
If he'd been like his former master, he'd have
knocked one back, but these days
wine was bitter and honey left
the aftertaste of nectar from his homeland –
he survived on bread and sorrow.

And here they were, still ruthless and hungry.
But he knew they'd been changed
in the way they carried their robes,
like the body's longing for a severed limb,
the jaw's ache for an absent tooth,
how they squinted during his questioning.

He could crush them,
squeeze them like dung beetles
into a brown and yellow mash,
and have his dark servants wash his hands.

But too many had suffered – it would end
with him. He would speak the truth in love
and say, "Yes, my brothers. It is I."

NAAMAN'S WIFE

How many years had she held the slave girl
captive, ordering her to wrap and unwrap
the stinking bandages from his arms

and face, ordering her not to speak
unless she spoke, while her lips
trembled a torrent of tears and bile,

of wanting to die every time he came home
from battle, and they lay in secret,
when she did what every good wife does –

buried her pride to satisfy his desire –
yet awakened each morning to search
every part of her body, fingering this mole,

that blemish, or her relief at the start
of her flow that they hadn't conceived
a bundle of scars? So when the slave girl

finally whispered the name of a prophet
in the land of her fathers, she urged him
out of her bosom to find in the desert

the source which became light, became
sound, became, in the waters of the Jordan,
the healed flesh of her husband.

MAGDALEN'S SONG

And what will happen to us
now that they have killed him?
Who will be there to tell us
never to bow, never to bend,
but to follow our star
out of our Gardens of Gethsemane?

We walked with him on the way,
but not to be free like this,
with his mother broken
when she saw his body
hanging from a tree,
digging her finger in the dirt,
as if by burying her tears,
she could bring him back from the dead?

And now there's no one left
except her, the boy, and me –
the men deserted him – and Romans
who knew I would have died beside him
when they held their swords to my throat,
and looked in my eyes and laughed,
not because they wouldn't have killed me,
but they had known me before
as the woman with seven demons,
but now I was only a woman
looking up at a dead man –
black wings hovering behind the clouds.

MAGDALEN IN THE GARDEN

I went to the tomb with the other women,
our hands limp as the rags
we carried to wash away dried blood

from his eyes, ears, feet, and flesh,
to anoint his body with oils,
with prayers as final as the stone

we expected at the mouth of the cave,
with no one to help us –
not even the boy who laid him out,

and blessed his body with a threadbare sheet
to cover his nakedness until we returned.
But now the boy wouldn't accompany us

out of fear of those who have always
stood between us and our joy.
And then this man whom I mistook

for another, until I heard his voice
and realized it was He –
who had never listened

when we called ourselves blind,
deaf, crippled, leprous, or lost,
but always saw us as whole,
and called us into abundant life.

SUNDAY HOMILY

She had me singing psalms on Sunday
morning before the call to prayer,
the reading of her feet, calves, thighs

and exhortation to reach higher
to partake the wafer of her tongue,
wine of her lips, babbling the language

of angels with the homily to become one –
no closing hymn as triumphant
no communion as complete.

THANKSGIVING SESTINA

(*For Nadia*)

At the centre of this house, I have lit a candle
to call back into my heart, my life, spirit
that enters my flesh with the sound of a drum,
the thin membrane in my chest that began the dance
we celebrate in the harvest we've kneaded into bread,
that we receive, bless, break, and serve with wine.

For no feast is complete without wine
that sets our flesh aglow, our bodies like bright candles,
quickening our cells like yeast fermenting bread,
growing beyond itself, the way our spirits
move outward to embrace lovers, and we dance
to the rhythm in our wrists, calves – echo of the drum

beat that shortens our lives – noise of the drum
born from bleats that tore morning air before wine
spilled hot on the ground, and later that night we danced,
ate, cured the hide around fires where our candles
sparked, joining the round that draws spirit
to water, to fragrance in the mystery of bread –

music of crushed seeds, folded into loaves of bread
held between our palms like the *toom* of the drum
in the trembling altar of my shoulders, signal of spirit
coiling up the snake of my spine, like gladdening wine
exploding inside my head, a thousand candles
ablaze behind my eyes and I rise and dance.

For how can I resist the pull of this dance?
Unseen yet felt, like the miracle of bread
made real in our hands, the way candles
awaken our bodies to fire in the skin of drums,
in the pulp of grapes we squeeze into wine
surrendering their essence like spirit

anointing our bones and hearts (for spirit
sanctifies clenched fists and open hands) in the dance
of earth, air, and water, fluid as wine
poured into our lives, leavening hurts and loves like bread
made in the heat of fire, cooled by drums,
the song of our souls, like the breath of candles.

So I will cup my body around this candle and dance.
Give thanks to the spirit with music, bread
and wine, fruits of the earth, made one with the drum.

A PRAYER FOR MY CHILDREN

When you find yourself in a faraway land
surrounded by men, animals that mutter strange
sounds, do not be afraid: neither you, your parents,

nor your ancestors have ever been alone.
So trust the earth to bear you up, follow
the wind as it leads you through valleys

clustered with trees heavy with fruit –
some that seem familiar enough to eat,
but you still aren't sure they are the same

as the ones you left on the other side
of the river that you've now forgotten.
Eat. Feast on the bounty. Feed the fire

that burns away the knot in your stomach,
sets ablaze the horizon, all that your eyes
can see – that has been promised

to you since your cry pierced the morning air:
your parents bathed you with kisses,
baptized you with caresses,

swaddled you in care before you uttered
your first words to the moon, sun, stars,
wobbled your first steps into unknowing –

all the while rising into your inheritance.
And if you awaken under the branches of a cotton
tree, cradled in its roots, draw a circle around

yourself and all those whom you love, cross
yourself three times before you step over
the threshold. Welcome the ancestors,

all the kindly spirits who have followed you,
your parents across many seas, oceans,
and deserts; entertain them with strong drink

and soft food: rice, yams, bananas, the ever
present rum to bless the hands that have lifted
you up, and sanctified the place you now call home.

LIVICATIONS

Dub Wise has been a journey of understanding and giving back. The shaping of this collection began with the insights of rocksteady, reggae, and *dubwise*: the pared down essentials of drum and bass after which there is only the silence from which it emerged. Rocksteady and reggae have the ability to combine, as Kwame Dawes has contended, the erotic, socio-economic, political, and spiritual into an aesthetic experience. *Dubwise* suggests plenitude and the reclamation of subjectivity through the vehicle of the body. I have learned this from listening, loving, and dancing to this uncertain music.

So, give thanks to the poets, prophets, players and arrangers of instruments who've made the "tradition" *Irie*: Alton Ellis, The Techniques, The Heptones, The Paragons, John Holt, Delroy Wilson, Phyllis Dillon, The Melodians, Ken Boothe, King Tubby, Sir "Coxone" Dodd, Lee "Scratch" Perry, Big Youth, Junior Byles, Bob Andy, Duke Reid, Burning Spear and The Wailers: Bunny, Peter, and Bob. The more I listened to the music and the individual stamp that these singers brought to the music, the more I became convinced of my own need to find my voice in my vocation.

I first heard the grumble of this subversive music on a turntable that my mother, Merty Philp (nee Lumley) played on Saturday evenings. When she abandoned her records for the church, I inherited her 45s and LPs. As I grew older, I expanded my listening in the homes of my friends: Paul Smith, David "Griffo" Griffiths, Paul "Pat Chow" Chin, Danny and Joan Morrison, Michael Boothe, and Jah Mick, where the fat bass lines came tumbling out the twin eighteen inch speakers on his verandah. And I can't forget Michael Witter, who introduced me to the work of Gil Scott-Heron, The Last Poets, jazz, and the music of the African diaspora. But that is for another volume.

Then came the Word. The teachers from whom I learned how to give back in verse: Dennis Scott, Anthony McNeill, Mervyn Morris, Lorna Goodison, Edward Baugh, Olive Senior, Pam Mordecai, Kamau Brathwaite and Derek Walcott. There have been others, but these formed the bedrock on which I could *overstand* my relationship with language and extending the conversation of these elders.

As I've learned and trod, I met a beautiful woman, Nadezka, whom I would marry and we'd have three wonderful children: Anna, Christina, and Andrew. I love them dearly and they have returned that love in many ways. Their presence has led me to realizations that I wouldn't have known had I remained apart from their lives. As the saying goes, I know I would "take a bullet for them."

This give and take of commitment has also helped me to recognize and include my family and my wife's family – too many to name individually. But I would be remiss if I did not mention the matriarch, Anatolia Patino (nee Salazar), who has stood by us like a guardian angel through difficulties and triumphs.

Give thanks also to the other angels. In my professional life at Miami Dade College where I have earned my keep for thirty years: Dr. Eduardo Padron, Dr. Jose Vicente, Dean Harry Hoffman, Josett Peat, Ken Boos, Gina Cortes-Suarez, Preston Allen, Mervyn Solomon, Joe McNair, and Alina Interian. And in my writing and virtual life: Judith Foster, Richard Philp, Tathiana Patino, Francisco Patino, Rethabile Masilo, Sandra Castillo, Lisa Day-Lindsay, Lou Skellings, Malou Harrison, Malachi Smith, Nicolette Bethel, Stephen Bess, Randy Baker, Kevin McLaughlin, Donna Aza Weir-Soley, Heather Russell, Barrington Salmon, Michelle McGrane, Fragano Ledgister, Janine Mendes-Franco, Robert Hruzek, Andrene Bonner, Jacqueline Bishop, Sheron Hamilton-Pearson, Sokari Ekine, and Nicholas Laughlin.

Finally, I must give thanks to Jeremy Poynting and Hannah Bannister, who throughout the years have supported not only my work, but the work of many other Caribbean writers. The Caribbean owes you a debt of gratitude.

Geoffrey Philp
Miami, Florida
February 2010

ABOUT THE AUTHOR

Geoffrey Philp writes:

'I was born in Kingston, Jamaica, and I attended Mona Primary and Jamaica College, where I studied literature under the tutelage of Dennis Scott. When I left Jamaica in 1979, I went to Miami Dade College and after graduating, I studied Caribbean, African and African-American literature with Dr. O.R. Dathorne and creative writing with Lester Goran, Evelyn Wilde Mayerson, and Isaac Bashevis Singer. Since then, I have attended workshops with Derek Walcott , Edward Albee, and Israeli playwright, Matti Meged. As a James Michener Fellow at the University of Miami, I studied poetry under Kamau Brathwaite and fiction with George Lamming.

In 1990, I published my first book of poems, *Exodus and Other Poems,* and four other poetry collections have followed: *Florida Bound (1985), hurricane center (1998), xango music (2001)*, and *Twelve Poems and A Story for Christmas (2005)*. I have also written two books of short stories, *Uncle Obadiah and the Alien (1997)* and *Who's Your Daddy?* (2009), and a novel, *Benjamin, My Son (2003)* which was set in Jamaica during the turbulent eighties – a time of gang and class warfare, mass exodus, and the emergence of reggae, Rastafari and Bob Marley. I published a children's book, *Grandpa Sydney's Anancy Stories in 2009*, and I'm working on a novel, *Miami Lovesong*, which is set in South Florida. The major stars of the novel are a hurricane, a missing daughter, and a Rastaman – kind of Zora Neale Hurston meets South Florida and Jamaica.

My poems and short stories have appeared in *Small Axe*, *Asili*, *The Caribbean Writer*, *Gulf Stream*, *Florida in Poetry: A History of the Imagination*, *Wheel and Come Again: An Anthology of Reggae Poetry*, *Whispers from the Cotton Tree Root*, *The Oxford Book of Caribbean Short Stories*, and *The Oxford Book of Caribbean Verse*.'

Geoffrey Philp has a popular Caribbean blogspot:
http://geoffreyphilp.blogspot.com

POETRY BY GEOFFREY PHILP

Florida Bound
ISBN: 9780948833823; pp. 64; pub. 1995; £7.99

Geoffrey Philp was born and grew up in Jamaica. He now lives in Miami. His poems of exasperation and longing explore a reluctance to leave Jamaica and the 'marl-white roads at Struie' and anger that 'blackman still can't live in him own/black land' where 'gunman crawl like bedbug'. But whilst poems explore the keeness and sorrows of an exile's memory, the new landscape of South Florida landscape fully engages the poet's imagination. The experience of journeying is seen as part of a larger pattern of restless but creative movement in the Americas. Philp joins other Caribbean poets in making use of nation language, but few have pushed the collision between roots language and classical forms to greater effect.

Carrol Fleming writes in *The Caribbean Writer*: 'His poems are as vibrant and diverse as Miami where "each street crackles with dialects/variegated as the garish crotons". Miami, albeit citified, becomes just one more island with all that is good, bad and potentially violent beset by the same sea, same hurricanes, and "mangroves lashed sapless by the wind".

"Philp's poems wander through bedrooms and along the waterfronts of that perceptive land accessible only to poets, only to those who can pull the day through dawn fog to the delicate "breath of extinguished candles".

Hurricane Center
ISBN: 9781900715232; pp. 67; pub. 1998; £7.99

El nino stirs clouds over the Pacific. Flashing TV screens urge a calm that no one believes. The police beat a slouched body, crumpled like a fist of kleenex. The news racks are crowded with stories of pestilence, war and rumours of war. The children, once sepia-faced cherubim, mutate to monsters that eat, eat, eat. You notice a change in your body's conversation with itself, and in the garden the fire ants burrow into the flesh of the fruit.

Geoffrey Philps's poems stare into the dark heart of a world where hurricanes, both meteorological and metaphorical, threaten you to the last cell. But the sense of dread also reveals what is most precious in life, for the dark and accidental are put in the larger context of season and human renewal, and *Hurricane Center* returns always to the possibilities of redemption and joy.

In the voices of Jamaican prophets, Cuban exiles, exotic dancers, drunks, race-track punters, canecutters, rastamen, middle-class householders and screw-face ghetto sufferers, Geoffrey Philp writes poetry which is both intimately human and cosmic in scale. On the airwaves between Miami and Kingston, the rhythms of reggae and mambo dance through these poems.

Xango Music
ISBN: 9781900715461; pp. 64; pub. 2001; £7.99

In the Xango ceremony, the contraries of New World African experience find transcendence. From the established, bodily patterns of ritual comes release into the freedom of the spirit; from the exposure of pain comes the possibilities of healing; and for the individual there is both the dread aloneness with the gods and the 'we-ness' of community.

Simultaneously the rites celebrate the rich, syncretic diversity, the multiple connections of the African person in the New World and enact the tragic search for the wholeness of the lost African centre. And there is the god himself, standing at the crossroads, 'beating iron into the shape of thunder', both the prophetic voice warning of the fire to command the creator who hammers out sweet sound from the iron drum.

Geoffrey Philp finds in Xango a powerful metaphor that is both particular to the Caribbean and universal in its relevance.

David and Phyllis Gershator writes in *The Caribbean Writer*: 'Using rhythm and riffs, he can pull the stops on language and give it a high energy kick. In 'jam-rock' he winds up with 'the crack of bones, the sweat of the whip; girl, you gonna get a lot of it; get it galore; my heart still beats uncha, uncha uncha, cha'.